Software Requirements Specification (SRS) 2.0

--The Structure-Behavior Coalescence Approach--

William S. Chao

2

Structure-Behavior Coalescence

$$\text{Software Architecture} = \text{Software Structure} + \text{Software Behavior}$$

4

CONTENTS

PREFACE

Software requirements specification (SRS) is, in the software development process, a result of the requirements and specifications phase. That is, a software requirements specification is for the analysts to find out what the customers indeed expect the software system to do for them. When working on the software requirements specification, we only specify what this software system is, but never ask how this software system shall be manufactured.

A software system has been specified, by software requirements specification (SRS) 1.0, hopefully to be an integrated whole, embodied in its assembled components, their interactions with each other and the environment. Since software structure and software behavior are the two most prominent views of software systems, integrating software structure and software behavior is clearly the best way to achieve truly integrated software systems. Because software requirements specification 1.0 does not specify the integration of software structure and software behavior, very likely it will never be able to actually form an integrated whole of a software system.

Structure-behavior coalescence (SBC) provides an elegant way to integrate the software structure and software behavior, and hence achieves a truly integrated whole, of a software system. A truly integrated whole sets a path to achieve the desired software requirements specification (SRS). SBC facilitates an integrated whole. Therefore, we conclude that software requirements specification (SRS) 2.0 using the SBC approach, which contains three fundamental diagrams: a) architecture hierarchy diagram, b) component operation diagram and c) interaction flow diagram, is highly adequate in specifying a software system.

ABOUT THE AUTHOR

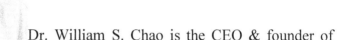Dr. William S. Chao is the CEO & founder of SBC Architecture International®. SBC (Structure-Behavior Coalescence) architecture is a systems architecture which demands the integration of systems structure and systems behavior of a system. SBC architecture applies to hardware architecture, software architecture, enterprise architecture, knowledge architecture and thinking architecture. The core theme of SBC architecture is: "Architecture = Structure + Behavior".

William S. Chao received his bachelor degree (1976) in telecommunication engineering and master degree (1981) in information engineering, both from the National Chiao-Tung University, Taiwan. From 1976 till 1983, he worked as an engineer at Chung-Hwa Telecommunication Company, Taiwan.

William S. Chao received his master degree (1985) in information science and Ph.D. degree (1988) in information science, both from the University of Alabama at Birmingham, USA. From 1988 till 1991, he worked as a computer scientist at GE Research and Development Center, Schenectady, New York, USA.

PART I: BASIC CONCEPTS

Chapter 1: Introduction to Software Requirements Specification

A software requirements specification (SRS) has traditionally been viewed as a document that communicates the requirements of the customer to the technical community who will specify and build the software system.

For the SRS approach to specify a software system as an integrated whole of that software system's multiple views, it must be able to integrate the software structure and system behavior when specifying a system.

Current multiple views non-integrated approaches for software requirements specification 1.0 such as function-oriented, behavioral and object-oriented, more or less, fail to specify a software system as an integrated whole of that software system's multiple views because they are not able to integrate the software structure and software behavior when specifying a software system.

Multiple views integrated approaches for software requirements specification 2.0, such as SBC, provide a sophisticated way to integrate the software structure and software behavior when specifying a software system.

1-1 Software Development Process

A software systems development carries out the work flow steps and therefore may also be called software development process [Pres09, Somm06, Your99]. We need to define a software development process in order to engineer a software system correctly from start to finish. The software development process, as shown in Figure 1-1, can be divided into five phases: a) project planning, b) requirements and specifications, c) design and implementation, d) verification and validation and e) product evolution.

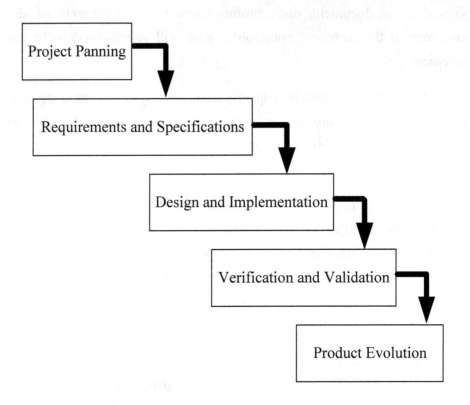

Figure 1-1   Five Phases of the Software Development Process

1-1-1 Project Planning

Project planning determines the general goals of the software development project. These general goals include: project scope determination; selection of the software process model; selection of the software engineering development technology; estimating applicable resources; determining software metric methodology; cost estimation; risk management; project scheduling and tracking; determining the configuration management approach; understanding the level of quality management; choosing software engineering tools; drawing up contracts; and determining post-project follow up.

1-1-2 Requirements and Specifications

The requirements and specifications phase consists of determining what the customer really requires. Requirements and specifications appertain to the problem space. When working on requirements and specifications, we usually only specify what the software system is, but never think about how this software system shall be manufactured.

1-1-3 Design and Implementation

The design and implementation phase belongs to the solution space. In other words, design and implementation try to secure a solution to meet or exceed customer requirements. It is opposite to requirements and specifications, design and implementation mainly consider how to manufacture this software system, but not to specify what this software system is.

1-1-4 Verification and Validation

The fourth step is called the verification and validation, abbreviated as V&V, phase. Verification uses proving technology. Validation uses testing technology. After the software product has been manufactured, we use either verification or validation to determine if or not the software product meets the requirements and specifications initially settled.

1-1-5 Product Evolution

Product evolution is the fifth, also the last, phase of software process. After verification and validation, we hand over the software product for the customer to use. Uses for several years, several month or even several days later, if has the necessity to carry on the next edition, either perceive that some part of wrong, some parts need the reinforcement, either the customer thinks that some places must change the requirements and specifications, even overhauls greatly, then must carry on the product evolution in accordance.

1-2 Software Requirements Specification

Software requirements specification (SRS) is, in the software development process, the requirements and specifications phase [Lapl13, Rinz09, Wieg13]. That is, a software requirements specification is for the analysts to find out what the customers indeed expect the software system to do for them. When working on the software requirements specification, we only specify what this software system is, but never ask how this software system shall be manufactured.

During the requirements and specifications phase, both customers and analysts need to coordinate closely, exchange the opinion fully, finally achieve the specifications document output, as shown in Figure 1-2.

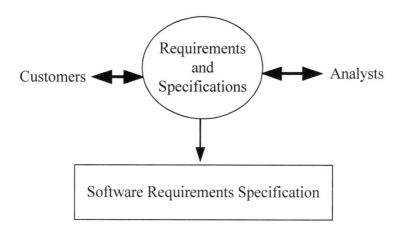

Figure 1-2   Work of Requirements and Specifications

Customers maintain great responsibility in the requirements and specifications work. The opinion and request on the software system provided by the customer can be the very precious primitive information in the software requirements specification. Therefore, customers need to coordinate closely with analysts during the work of requirements and specifications.

Analysts also uphold magnificent responsibility in the requirements and specifications work. The analyst must be able to grasp specialized knowledge on computer hardware, firmware and software, is good at carrying on the abstract logical thinking and the creative thinking, can listen attentively to others' opinion. In addition, the analyst also is liable to assemble the software specifications document.

1-3 Multiple Views of a Software System

In general, a software system is extremely complex that it consists of multiple views such as structure view, behavior view, function view, data view as shown in Figure 1-3 [Denn08, Kend10, Pres09, Somm06].

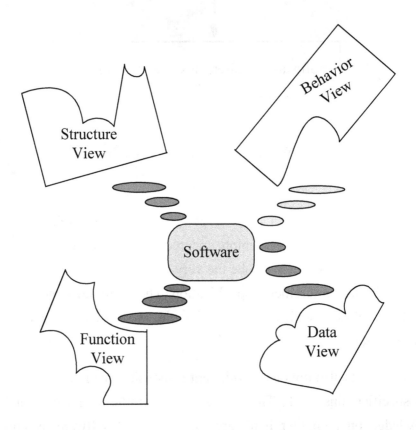

Figure 1-3   Multiple Views of a Software System

Among the above multiple views, the structure and behavior views are perceived as the two prominent ones. The structure view focuses on the software structure which is described by components and their composition while the behavior view concentrates on the software behavior which involves interactions [Chao15a, Chao15b, Chao15c, Chao15d, Chao15e, Hoar85, Miln89, Miln99] among the external environment's actors and components. Function and data views are considered to be other views as shown in Figure 1-4.

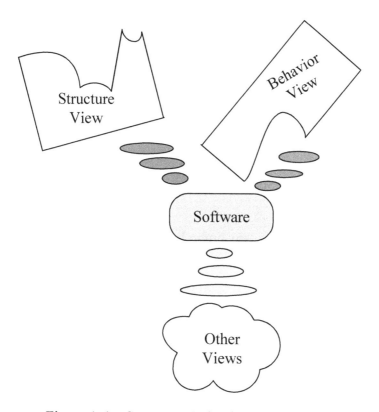

Figure 1-4   Structure, Behavior and Other Views

Either Figure 1-3 or Figure 1-4 represents the multiple views of a software system. In some situations Figure 1-3 is used and in other situations Figure 1-4 is used.

Accordingly, a software system is specified in Figure 1-5 to be an integrated whole of that software's multiple views, i.e., structure, behavior and other views, embodied in its assembled components, their interactions [Chao15a, Chao15b, Chao15c, Chao15d, Chao15e, Hoar85, Miln89, Miln99] with each other and the environment. Components are sometimes labeled as non-aggregated systems, parts, entities, objects and building blocks [Chao14a, Chao14b, Chao14c].

> A software system is an integrated whole of that software's multiple views, i.e., structure, behavior, and other views, embodied in its assembled components, their interactions with each other and the environment.

Figure 1-5   Specification of a Software System

Since multiple views are embodied in the software's assembled components which belong to the software structure, they shall not exist alone. Multiple views must be loaded on the software structure just like a cargo is loaded on a ship as shown in Figure 1-6. There will be no multiple views if there is no software structure. Stand-alone multiple views are not meaningful.

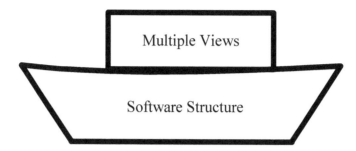

Figure 1-6   Multiple Views Loaded on the Software Structure

1-4 Multiple Views Non-Integrated Approaches for Software Requirements Specification 1.0

When specifying a software system, the multiple views non-integrated approach, also known as the model multiplicity approach [Dori95, Dori02, Dori16], respectively picks a model for each view as shown in Figure 1-7, the structure view has the structure model; the behavior view has the behavior model; the function view has the function model; the data view has the data model. These multiple models, are heterogeneous and not related to each other, and thus become the primary cause of model multiplicity problems [Dori95, Dori02, Dori16, Pele02, Sode03].

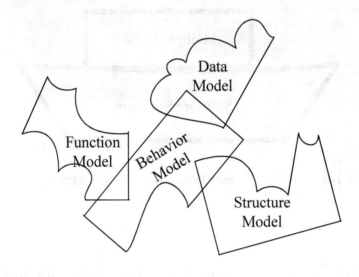

Figure 1-7   Multiple Views Non-Integrated Approach

Multiple views non-integrated approaches for software requirements specification 1.0 fall into three general categories: function-oriented, behavioral and object-oriented [Laue02, Rinz09], as shown in Figure 1-8. Each of these approaches, more or less, fails to describe a software system as an integrated whole of that software's multiple views.

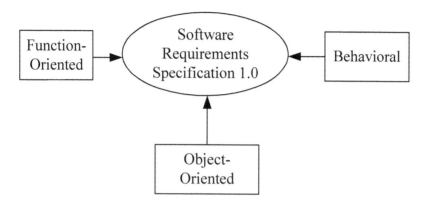

Figure 1-8   Multiple Views Non-Integrated Approaches
for Software Requirements Specification (SRS) 1.0

Function-oriented approaches for software requirements specification (SRS) 1.0 organize the requirements into hierarchies of functions that communicate via data flows. Each function is represented by a transformation from input data to output data. A software system may contain many such kinds of functions which represent the function view of the software system. Classical Structured Analysis (SA) [DeMa79] fits into the category of function-oriented methods, as do Structured Analysis and Design Technique (SADT) [Marc88] and Structured Systems Analysis and Design Method (SSADM) [Ashw90]. Function-oriented approaches concentrate only on the function view and completely neglect to integrate the software structure and software behavior. Therefore, function-oriented approaches are multiple views non-integrated and will never become an ideal SRS approach.

Behavioral approaches for software requirements specification (SRS) 1.0 describe external behavior of the software in terms of some notions, mathematical functions, or state machines. Petri Net [Reis92] and flowcharting [Bash86] are primarily behavioral. Behavioral approaches concentrate only on the behavior view and completely neglect to integrate the software structure and software behavior. Just like process-based approaches, behavioral approaches are multiple views non-integrated and will never become an ideal SRS approach.

Object-oriented approaches for software requirements specification (SRS) 1.0 specify the system as classes of objects and their behaviors. Object-oriented Analysis (OOA) [Booc07], fitting into the category of object-oriented methods, looks at the problem domain, with the aim of producing a conceptual model of the information that exists in the area being analyzed. The result of object-oriented analysis is a description of what the system is behaviorally required to do, in the form of a conceptual model. That will typically be presented as a set of use cases and a number of activity diagrams. Object-oriented approaches stress both the structure view and the behavior view, but not an integrated structure and behavior views. Object-oriented approaches do not emphasize to integrate the software structure and software behavior. Like process-based and behavioral approaches, object-oriented approaches are multiple views non-integrated and will never become an ideal SRS approach.

1-5 Multiple Views Integrated Approaches for Software Requirements Specification 2.0

When specifying a software system, the multiple views integrated approach, also known as the model singularity approach [Dori95, Dori02, Dori16, Pele02, Sode03], instead of picking many heterogeneous and unrelated models, will use only one single model as shown in Figure 1-9. The structure, behavior, function and data views are all integrated in this one single model which represents an integrated whole of that system's multiple views [Chao14a, Chao14b, Chao14c].

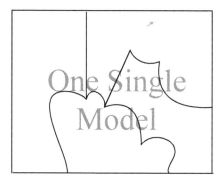

Figure 1-9   Multiple Views Integrated Approach

Multiple views integrated approaches for software requirements specification (SRS) 2.0 specify a software system as an integrated whole of that software's multiple views.

Chapter 2: Software Structure and Software Behavior

Software structure and software behavior are the two most significant views of a software system. Software structure, specified by components, their operations and their composition, refers to the type of connection between the components of a software system. Software behavior, specified by the interactions between and among the components and environment, refers to the interconnectivities a software system in conjunction with its environment.

2-1 Software Structure

Every software system forms a whole. In general, software structure is the type of connection between the components of a software system. More specifically, we specify the software structure by 1) components, 2) their operations and 3) their composition.

Components are something relatively indivisible in one software system [Hoff10, Shel11]. For example, *PurchaseInput_UI*, *PurchasePrint_UI* and *Purchase_Database* are components of the *Purchase System* as shown in Figure 2-1.

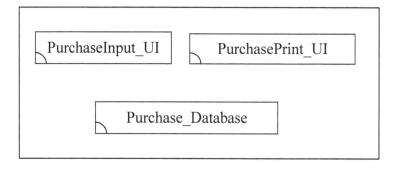

Figure 2-1   Components of the *Purchase System*

An operation provided by each component represents a procedure or method or function of the component [Chao14a, Chao14b, Chao14c]. Each component in a system must possess at least one operation. Figure 2-2 shows the operations of all components of the *Purchase_System*. In the figure, component *PurchaseInput_GUI* has one operation: *PurchaseDataInput*; component *PurchasePrint_GUI* has one operation: *PurchasePrintButtonClick*; component *Purchase_Database* has two operations: *Sql_p_insert* and *Sql_p_select*.

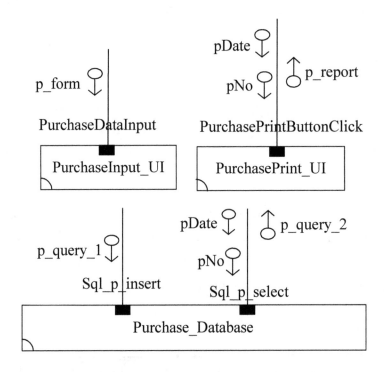

Figure 2-2   Operations of all Components of
the *Purchase System*

Composition of components designs the structural composition and decomposition of a system. For example, Figure 2-3 shows that, in the *Purchase System, Purchase_System* is composed of *Presentation_Layer* and *Data_Layer*; *Presentation_Layer* is composed of *PurchaseInput_UI* and *PurchasePrint_UI*; *Data_Layer* is composed of *Purchase_Database*.

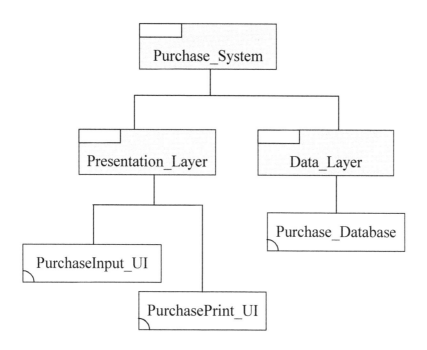

Figure 2-3   Structural Composition of
the *Purchase_System*

2-2 Software Behavior

Systems behavior refers to the interactions a software system in conjunction with its environment. It is the response of a software system to various stimuli, whether internal or external, conscious or subconscious, overt or covert, and voluntary or involuntary.

For example, Figure 2-4 demonstrates two individual behaviors: *PurchaseInput* and *PurchasePrint* that refer to the interactions the *Purchase System* in conjunction with its environment.

For each behavior, the environment always initiates the interaction and will lead more follow-up interactions to be realized among components. For example, Figure 2-5 demonstrates that interactions between and among the environment and the *PurchaseInput_UI*, *Purchase_Database* components shall draw forth the *PurchaseInput* behavior.

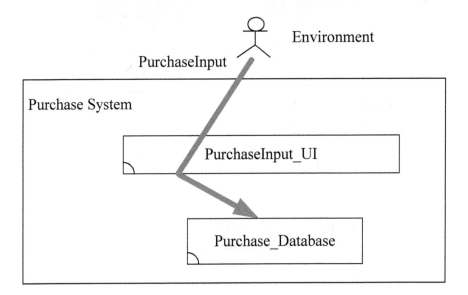

Figure 2-5   Interactions that Draw forth
the *PurchaseInput* Behavior

As a second example, Figure 2-6 demonstrates that interactions between and among the environment and the *PurchasePrint_UI*, *Purchase_Database* components shall draw forth the *PurchasePrint* behavior.

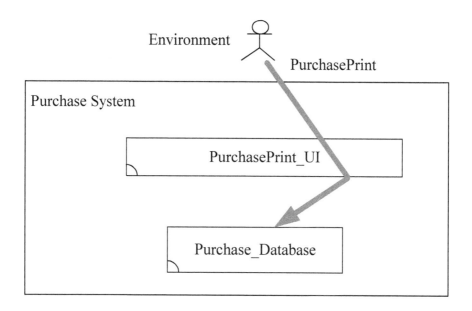

Figure 2-6   Interactions that Draw forth
the *OPurchasePrint* Behavior

Chapter 3: Structure-Behavior Coalescence

A software system has been specified hopefully to be an integrated whole, embodied in its assembled components, their interactions with each other and the environment. Since software structure and software behavior are the two most prominent views of a software system, integrating them apparently is the best way to achieve a truly integrated whole of a software system. Because software requirements specification 1.0 does not specify the integration of software structure and software behavior, very likely it will never be able to actually form an integrated whole of a software system.

Structure-behavior coalescence (SBC) provides an elegant way to integrate the software structure and software behavior, and hence achieves a truly integrated whole, of a software system. A truly integrated whole sets a path to achieve the desired software requirements specification (SRS). SBC facilitates an integrated whole. Therefore, we conclude that SBC sets a path to achieve the software requirements specification. Software requirements specification 2.0 uses the SBC approach and is highly adequate in specifying a software system.

3-1 Integrated Whole to Achieve the Software Requirements Specification

A software system has been specified hopefully to be an integrated whole, embodied in its assembled components, their interactions with each other and the environment. In other words, an integrated whole sets a path to achieve the software requirements specification (SRS) as shown in Figure 3-1.

36

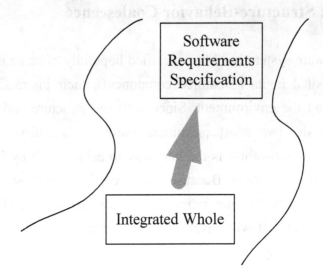

Figure 3-1   Integrated Whole to Achieve
the Software Requirements Specification

In one software requirements specification, different software structures may draw forth the same integrated whole as shown in Figure 3-2.

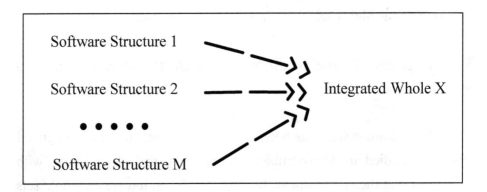

Figure 3-2   Different Software Structures Draw Forth
the Same Integrated Whole

Since there is only one software structure exists in one software requirements specification, one software structure will draw forth one integrated whole as shown in Figure 3-3.

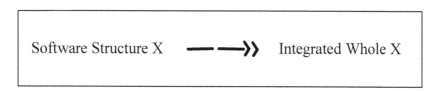

Figure 3-3   One Software Structure Draws Forth
One Integrated Whole

We conclude that in one software requirements specification, an integrated whole must be attached to or built on a software structure. In other words, an integrated whole shall not exist alone; it must be loaded on a software structure just like a cargo is loaded on a ship as shown in Figure 3-4. There will be no integrated whole if there is no software structure. A stand-alone integrated whole with no software structure is not meaningful.

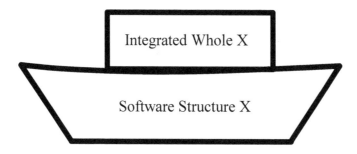

Figure 3-4   An Integrated Whole Must be Loaded on
a Software Structure

3-2 Integrating the Software Structure and Software Behavior

By integrating the software structures and software behaviors, we obtain structure-behavior coalescence (SBC) within a software system. Since software structures and software behaviors are so tightly integrated, we sometimes claim that the core theme of structure-behavior coalescence is: "Software Architecture = Software Structure + Software Behavior," as shown in Figure 3-5.

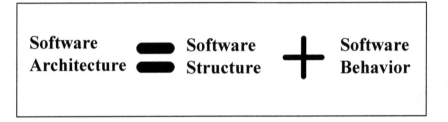

Figure 3-5   Core Theme of Structure-Behavior Coalescence

So far, integrating the software structure and software behavior has never been proposed or suggested besides the SBC approach. In most cases, software behaviors are separated from software structures when specifying a software system [Hoff10, Pres09, Shel11, Somm06].

3-3 Structure-Behavior Coalescence to Facilitate an Integrated Whole

Since software structure and software behavior are the two most prominent views of a software system, integrating them apparently is the best way to achieve a truly integrated whole of a software system. If we are not able to integrate the software structure and software behavior, then there is no way that we are able to integrate the whole software system. In other words, structure-behavior coalescence (SBC) facilitates a truly integrated whole as shown in Figure 3-6.

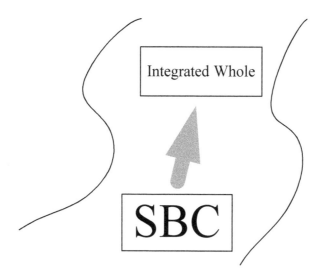

Figure 3-6   SBC Facilitates an Integrated Whole

Since software requirements specification 1.0 does not specify the integration of software structure and software behavior, very likely it will never be able to actually form an integrated whole of a software system. In this situation, software requirements specification 1.0 is powerless in specifying a software system adequately.

3-4 Structure-Behavior Coalescence to Achieve the Software Requirements Specification

Figure 3-1 declares that an integrated whole sets a path to achieve the desired software requirements specification. Figure 3-6 declares that structure-behavior coalescence facilitates a truly integrated whole.

Combining the above two declarations, we conclude that the structure-behavior coalescence (SBC) approach sets a path to achieve the software requirements specification as shown in Figure 3-7.

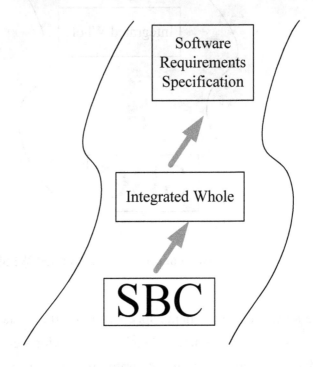

Figure 3-7   SBC to Achieve
the Software Requirements Specification

In the SBC approach, different software structures may draw forth the same software behavior as shown in Figure 3-8.

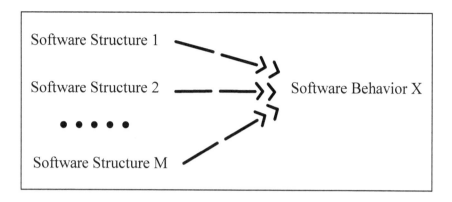

Figure 3-8   Different Software Structures Draw Forth
the Same Software Behavior

Since there is only one software structure exists in one software
requirements specification, one software behavior will always be attached
to or built on one software structure as shown in Figure 3-9.

Software Structure X   ——→》 Software Behavior X

Figure 3-9   One Software Behavior is Attached to
One Software Structure

We conclude that in the SBC approach, a software behavior must
be attached to or built on a software structure. In other words, a software
behavior can not exist alone; it must be loaded on a software structure

just like a cargo is loaded on a ship as shown in Figure 3-10. There will be no software behavior if there is no software structure. A stand-alone software behavior with no software structure is not meaningful.

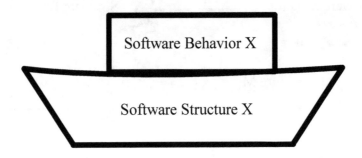

Figure 3-10   A Software Behavior Must be Loaded on
a Software Structure

3-5 SBC Method for Software Requirements Specification 2.0

Since structure-behavior coalescence (SBC) provides an elegant way to integrate the software structure and software behavior, we shall include it in the specification of a software system. Figure 3-11 shows how the software requirements specification 2.0 specifies a software system.

> A software system,
> through the SBC approach,
> truly is an integrated whole,
> embodied in its assembled components,
> their interactions with each other and the environment.

Figure 3-11   Software Requirements Specification 2.0
Specifying a Software System

A software system specified by the software requirements specification 2.0 has the following characteristics: 1) it emphasizes the software system's structure-behavior coalescence; 2) it is a truly integrated whole; 3) it is embodied in its assembled components; 4) components are interacting (or handshaking) [Chao15a, Chao15b, Chao15c, Chao15d, Chao15e, Hoar85, Miln89, Miln99] with each other and the environment; and 5) it uses structural decomposition [Chao14a, Chao14b, Chao14c, Ghar11] rather than functional decomposition [Scho10].

Structure-behavior coalescence (SBC) provides an elegant way to integrate the software structure and software behavior of a software system. Software requirements specification 2.0 uses the SBC approach to formally specify the integration of software structure and software behavior of a software system. Software requirements specification 2.0 contains three fundamental diagrams: a) architecture hierarchy diagram, b) component operation diagram and c) interaction flow diagram.

So far, we have introduced the software requirements specification 2.0 which should be able to appropriately specify a software system. In the following chapters, we shall elaborate the details of the software requirements specification 2.0.

3-6 SBC Model Singularity

Channel-Based Single-Queue SBC Process Algebra (C-S-SBC-PA) [Chao17a], Channel-Based Multi-Queue SBC Process Algebra (C-M-SBC-PA) [Chao17b], Channel-Based Infinite-Queue SBC Process Algebra (C-I-SBC-PA) [Chao17c], Operation-Based Single-Queue SBC Process Algebra (O-S-SBC-PA) [Chao17d], Operation-Based Multi-Queue SBC Process Algebra (O-M-SBC-PA) [Chao17e] and Operation-Based Infinite-Queue SBC Process Algebra (O-I-SBC-PA) [Chao17f] are the six specialized SBC process algebras. The SBC process algebra (SBC-PA) shown in Figure 3-12 is a model singularity approach.

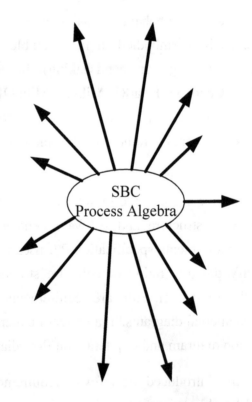

Figure 3-12   SBC-PA is a Model Singularity Approach.

The software requirements specification (SRS) 2.0 is also a model singularity approach. With SBC mind set sitting in the kernel, the SRS 2.0 single model shown in Figure 3-13 is therefore able to represent all structural views such as architecture hierarchy diagram (AHD), component operation diagram (COD), and behavioral views such as interaction flow diagram (IFD).

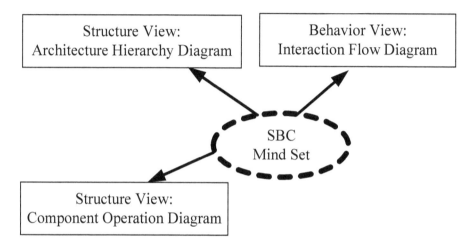

Figure 3-13   SRS 2.0 is a Model Singularity Approach.

The combination of SBC process algebra (SBC-PA) and software requirements specification (SRS) 2.0 is shown in Figure 3-14, again as a model singularity approach.

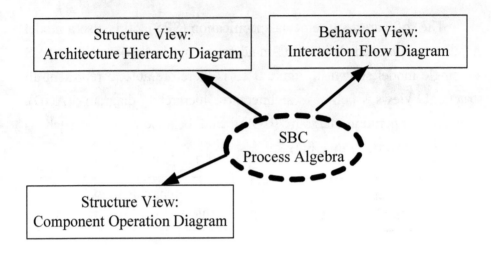

Figure 3-14   SBC Model is a Model Singularity Approach.

PART II: SBC APPROACH FOR SOFTWARE REQUIREMENTS SPECIFICATION 2.0

Chapter 4: Architecture Hierarchy Diagram

SBC approach for software requirements specification (SRS) 2.0 uses an architecture hierarchy diagram (AHD) to specify the multi-level decomposition and composition of a software system.

4-1 Decomposition and Composition

The following is an example of software decomposition and composition. The *Purchase_System* is composed of *Presentation_Layer* and *Data_Layer* as shown in Figure 4-1. *Presentation_Layer* and *Data_Layer* are subsystems comprising the *Purchase_System*.

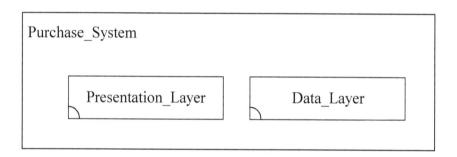

Figure 4-1   Decomposition and Composition of
the *Purchase_System*

Another example indicates that the *Sale_System* is composed of *Presentation_Layer* and *Data_Layer* as shown in Figure 4-2. *Presentation_Layer* and *Data_Layer* are subsystems comprising the *Sale_System*.

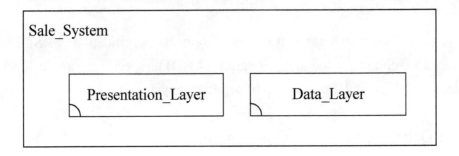

Figure 4-2   Decomposition and Composition of
the *Sale_System*

The architecture hierarchy diagram (AHD) is used to represent the decomposition and composition of a software system. As an example, an AHD of the *Purchase_System* is shown in Figure 4-3.

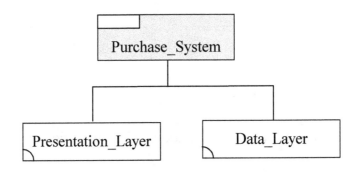

Figure 4-3   AHD of the *Purchase_System*

As a second example, Figure 4-4 shows an AHD of the *Sale_System*.

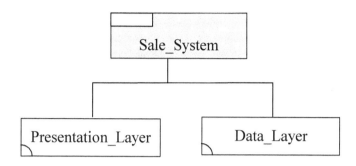

Figure 4-4   AHD of the *Sale_System*

4-2 Multi-Level Decomposition and Composition

The subsystem may also contain subsystems as we further decompose it. For example, *Presentation_Layer* is a subsystem of the *Purchase_System*, and we can further decompose it into *PurchaseInput_UI* and *PurchasePrint_UI*; *Data_Layer* is also a subsystem of the *Purchase_System*, and we can further decompose it into *Purchase_Database*, as shown in Figure 4-5.

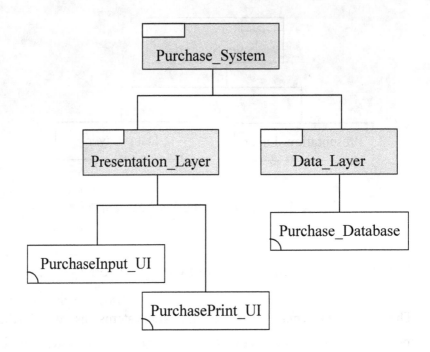

Figure 4-5   Multi-Level De/Composition of
the *Purchase System*

As a second example, *Presentation_Layer* is a subsystem of the *Sale_System*, and we can further decompose it into *SaleInput_UI* and *SalePrint_UI*; *Data_Layer* is also a subsystem of the *Sale_System*, and we can further decompose it into *Sale_Database*, as shown in Figure 4-6.

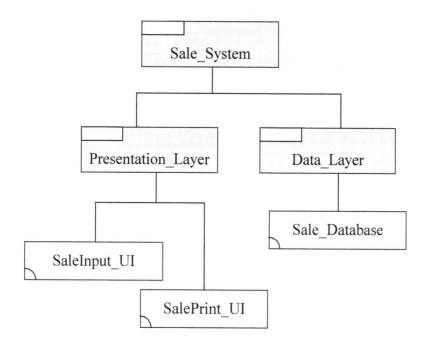

Figure 4-6   Multi-Level De/Composition of
the *Sale System*

4-3 Aggregated and Non-Aggregated Systems

Any system (at any level) involved with multi-level decomposition and composition of a software system is either aggregated or non-aggregated. The definition of aggregated and non-aggregated systems is shown in Figure 4-7.

Definition of Aggregated Systems:

A system (within an AHD) is aggregated if it is composed of any sub-system.

Definition of Non-aggregated Systems

A system (within an AHD) is non-aggregated if it is NOT composed of any sub-system.

Figure 4-7   Definition of Aggregated and
Non-aggregated Systems

Non-aggregated systems are sometimes referred to as components, parts, entities, objects and building blocks [Chao14a, Chao14b].

In the multi-level (hierarchical) decomposition and composition, any system is either aggregated or non-aggregated, but not both. For example, in Figure 4-3, *Presentation_Layer* is a non-aggregated system, not an aggregated system. As an interesting contrast, in Figure 4-5, *Presentation_Layer* is an aggregated system, not a non-aggregated system.

As a second example, in Figure 4-4, *Data_Layer* is a non-aggregated system, not an aggregated system. As an interesting contrast, in Figure 4-6, *Data_Layer* is an aggregated system, not a non-aggregated system.

Chapter 5: Component Operation Diagram

SBC approach for software requirements specification (SRS) 2.0 uses a component operation diagram (COD) to specify all components' operations of a software system.

5-1 Operations of Each Component

An operation provided by each component represents a procedure or method or function of the component. If other components request this component to perform an operation, then shall use it to accomplish the operation request.

Each component in a software system must possess at least one operation. A component should not exist in a software system if it does not possess any operation. Figure 5-1 shows that the *Purchase_Database* component has two operations: *Sql_p_insert* and *Sql_p_select*.

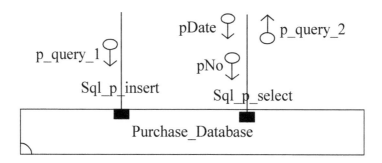

Figure 5-1   Two Operations of
the *Purchase_Database* Component

An operation formula is utilized to fully represent an operation. An operation formula includes a) operation name, b) input parameters and c) output parameters as shown in Figure 5-2.

$$\text{Operation\_Name (In } i_1, i_2, ..., i_m \text{ ; Out } o_1, o_2, ..., o_n \text{)}$$

Figure 5-2   Operation Formula

Operation name is the name of this operation. In a software system, every operation name should be unique. Duplicate operation names shall not be allowed in any software system.

An operation may have several input and output parameters. The input and output parameters, gathered from all operations, represent the input data and output data views of a software system [Date03, Elma10]. As shown in Figure 5-3, component *Purchase_Database* possesses the *Sql_p_insert* operation which has the *p_query_1* input parameter (with the arrow direction pointing to the component); component *Purchase_Database* also possesses the *Sql_p_select* operation which has the *pDate, pNo* input parameters (with the arrow direction pointing to the component) and the *p_query_2* output parameter (with the arrow direction opposite to the component).

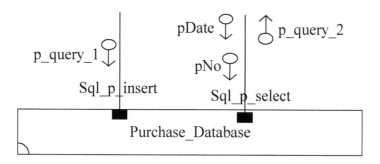

Figure 5-3   Input/Output Parameters

Data formats of input and output parameters can be described by data type specifications. There are two sets of data types: primitive and composite [Date03, Elma10]. Figure 5-4 shows the primitive data type specification of the *pDate* and *pNo* input parameters occurring in the *PurchasePrintButtonClick(In pDate, pNo; Out p_report)* and *Sql_p_select(In pDate, pNo; Out p_query_2)* operation formulas.

Parameter	Data Type	Instances
pDate	Text	20110317, 20110412
pNo	Text	003, 004

Figure 5-4   Primitive Data Type Specification

Figure 5-5 shows the composite data type specification of the *p_query_1* input parameter occurring in the *Sql_p_insert(In p_query_1)* operation formula.

Parameter	*p_query_1*

Data Type	TABLE of
	  Purchase Date : Text
	  Purchase No : Text
	  Supplier : Text
	  ProductNo : Text
	  Quantity : Integer
	  UnitPrice : Real
	  Total : Real
	End TABLE ;

Instances			

Purchase Date	Purchase No	Supplier	Total
20090230	001	Chao's Corp	1,080,000.00

ProductNo	Quantity	UnitPrice
A00001	1000	120.00
A00002	1000	220.00
A00003	1000	320.00
A00004	1000	420.00

Figure 5-5 Composite Data Type Specification of *p_query_1*

Figure 5-6 shows the composite data type specification of the *p_query_2* output parameter occurring in the *Sql_p_select(Out p_query_2)* operation formula.

Parameter	p_query_2

Data Type	TABLE of
	  Purchase Date : Text
	  Purchase No : Text
	  Supplier : Text
	  ProductNo : Text
	  Quantity : Integer
	  UnitPrice : Real
	  Total : Real
	End TABLE ;

Instances	(see table below)

Purchase Date	Purchase No	Supplier	Total
20090230	001	Chao's Corp	1,080,000.00

ProductNo	Quantity	UnitPrice
A00001	1000	120.00
A00002	1000	220.00
A00003	1000	320.00
A00004	1000	420.00

Figure 5-6   Composite Data Type Specification of *p_query_2*

5-2 Drawing the Component Operation Diagram

For a software system, COD is used to specify all components' operations. Figure 5-7 shows the *Purchase System's COD*. In the figure, component *PurchaseInput_GUI* has one operation: *PurchaseDataInput*; component *PurchasePrint_GUI* has one operation: *PurchasePrintButtonClick*; component *Purchase_Database* has two operations: *Sql_p_insert* and *Sql_p_select*.

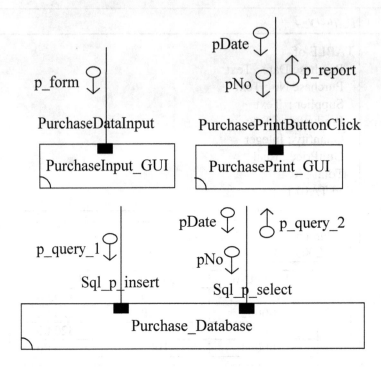

Figure 5-7   COD of the *Purchase System*

Chapter 6: Interaction Flow Diagram

SBC approach for software requirements specification (SRS) 2.0 uses an interaction flow diagram (IFD) to specify each individual behavior of the overall behavior of a software system.

6-1 Individual Behavior Represented by Interaction Flow Diagram

The overall behavior of a software system consists of many individual behaviors. Each individual behavior represents an execution path. An IFD is utilized to specify such an individual behavior.

Figure 6-1 demonstrates that the *Purchase System* has two behaviors; thus, it has two IFDs.

System	IFD
Purchase System	PurchaseInput
	PurchasePrint

Figure 6-1 *Purchase System* has Two IFDs

Figure 6-2 demonstrates that the *Sale System* has two behaviors; thus, it has two IFDs.

System	IFD
Sale System	SaleInput
	SalePrint

Figure 6-2 *Sale System* has Two IFDs

6-2 Drawing the Interaction Flow Diagram

Let us now explain the usage of interaction flow diagram (IFD) by drawing an IFD step by step. Figure 6-3 demonstrates an IFD of the *PurchaseInput* behavior. The X-axis direction is from the left side to right side and the Y-axis direction is from the above to the below. Inside an IFD, there are four elements: a) external environment's actor, b) components, c) interactions and d) input/output parameters. Participants of the interaction, such as the external environment's actor and each component, are laid aside along the X-axis direction on the top of the diagram. The external environment's actor which initiates the sequential interactions is always placed on the most left side of the X-axis. Then, interactions among the external environment's actor and components successively in turn decorate along the Y-axis direction. The first interaction is placed on the top of the Y-axis position. The last interaction is placed on the bottom of the Y-axis position. Each interaction may carry several input and/or output parameters.

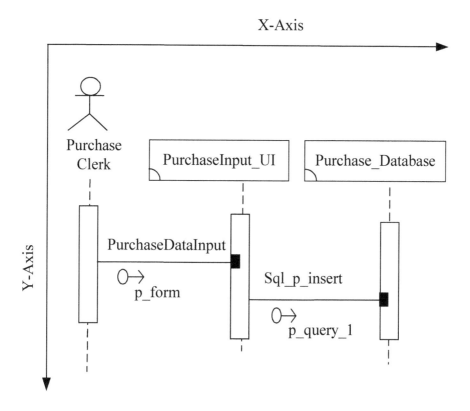

Figure 6-3   IFD of the *PurchaseInput* Behavior

In Figure 6-3, *Purchase Clerk* is an external environment's actor. *PurchaseInput_UI* and *Purchase_Database* are components. *PurchaseDataInput* is an operation, carrying the *p_form* input parameter, which is provided by the *PurchaseInput_UI* component. *Sql_p_insert* is an operation, carrying the *p_query_1* input parameter, which is provided by the *Purchase_Database* component.

The execution path of Figure 6-3 is as follows. First, actor *Purchase Clerk* interacts with the *PurchaseInput_UI* component through the *PurchaseDataInput* operation call interaction, carrying the *p_form* input parameter. Next, component *PurchaseInput_UI* interacts with the *Purchase_Database* component through the *Sql_p_insert* operation call interaction, carrying the *p_query_1* input parameter.

For each interaction, the solid line stands for operation call while the dashed line stands for operation return. The operation call and operation return interactions, if using the same operation name, belong to the identical operation. Figure 6-4 exhibits two interactions (operation call interaction and operation return interaction) having the identical "*PurchasePrintButtonClick*" operation.

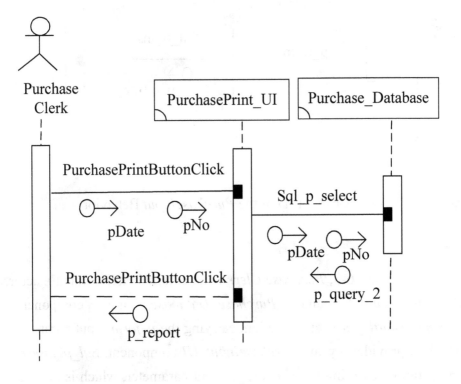

Figure 6-4   Two Interactions Have the Identical Operation

The execution path of Figure 6-4 is as follows. First, actor *Purchase Clerk* interacts with the *PurchasePrint_UI* component through the *PurchasePrintButtonClick* operation call interaction, carrying the *pDate* and *pNo* input parameters. Continuingly, component *PurchasePrint_UI* interacts with the *Purchase_Database* component through the *Sql_p_select* operation call interaction, carrying the *pDate* and *pNo* input parameters and the *p_query_2* output parameter. Finally, actor *Purchase Clerk* interacts with the *PurchasePrint_UI* component through the *PurchasePrintButtonClick* operation return interaction, carrying the *p_report* output parameter.

An interaction flow diagram may contain a conditional expression. Figure 6-5 shows such an example which has the following execution path. First, external environment's actor *Employee* interacts with the *Computer* component through the *Open* operation call interaction, carrying the *Task_No* input parameter. Next, if the *var_1* < 4 & *var_2* > 7 condition is true then component *Computer* shall interact with the *Skype* component through the *Op_1* operation call interaction and component *Skype* shall interact with the *Earphone* component through the *Op_4* operation call interaction, carrying the *Skype_Earphone* output parameter; else if the *var_3* = 99 condition is true then component *Computer* shall interact with the *Skype* component through the *Op_2* operation call interaction and component *Skype* shall interact with the *Speaker* component through the *Op_5* operation call interaction, carrying the *Skype_Speaker* output parameter; else component *Computer* shall interact with the *Youtube* component through the *Op_3* operation call interaction and component *Youtube* shall interact with the *Speaker* component through the *Op_6* operation call interaction, carrying the *Youtube_Speaker* output parameter. Continuingly, if the *var_1* < 4 & *var_2* > 7 condition is true then component *Computer* shall interact with the *Skype* component through the *Op_1* operation return interaction, carrying the *Status_1* output parameter; else if the *var_3* = *99* condition is true then component *Computer* shall interact with the *Skype* component through the *Op_2* operation return interaction, carrying the *Status_2* output parameter; else component *Computer* shall interact with the *Youtube* component through the *Op_3* operation return interaction, carrying the *Status_3* output parameter. Finally, external environment's actor *Employee* interacts with the *Computer* component through the *Open* operation return interaction, carrying the *Status* output parameter.

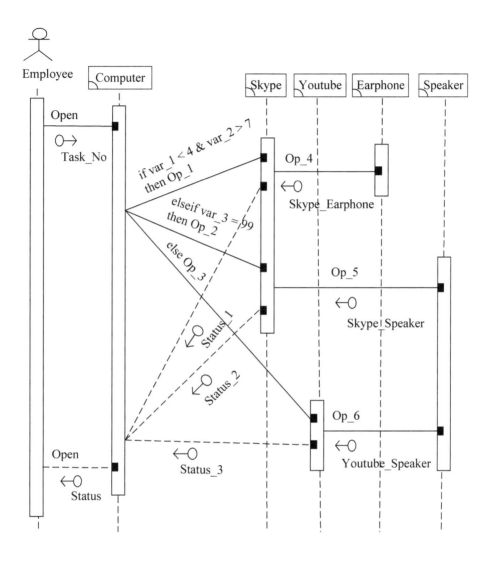

Figure 6-5   Conditional Interaction

Several Boolean conditions are shown in Figure 6-5. They are "*var_1 < 4 & var_2 > 7*" and "*var_3 = 99*". Variables, such as *var_1*, *var_2* and *var_3*, appearing in the Boolean condition can be local or global variables [Prat00, Seth96].

PART III: CASES STUDY

Chapter 7: Software Requirements Specification 2.0 of the Purchase System

This chapter examines the *Purchase System* which represents a case study of software requirements specification 2.0, using the structure-behavior coalescence approach. After the software development is finished, the overall behavior of the *Purchase System* is represented by two behaviors: *PurchaseInput* and *PurchasePrint* as shown in Figure 7-1.

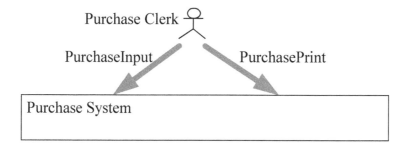

Figure 7-1   Two Behaviors of the *Purchase System*

In the *PurchaseInput* behavior, a purchase clerk uses the *PurchaseInput_GUI* component to input the purchase data, as shown in Figure 7-2.

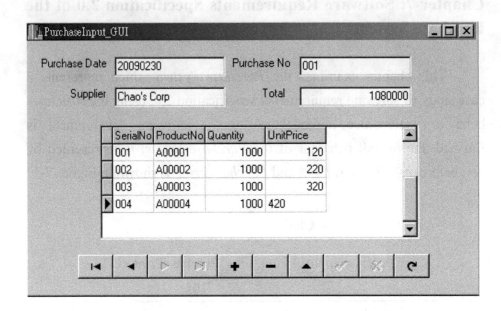

Figure 7-2   Input the Purchase Data

In the *PurchasePrint* behavior, a purchase clerk uses the *PurchasePrint_GUI* component to print out the purchase data, as shown in Figure 7-3.

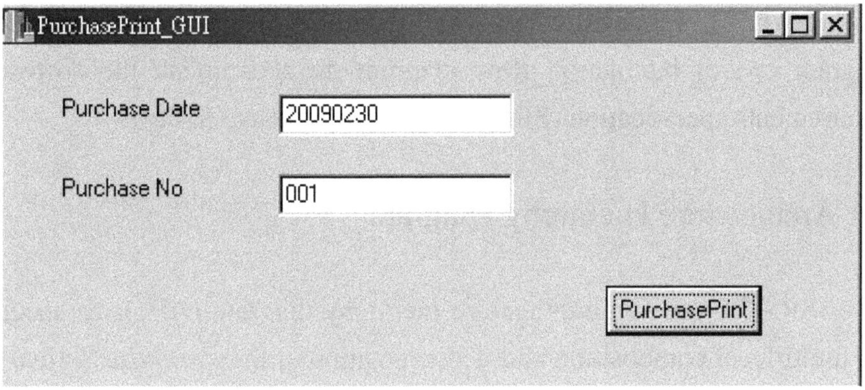

Figure 7-3   Print Out the Purchase Data

In Figure 7-3, a purchase clerk shall input the *Purchase Date* and *Purchase No* values first. After pressing down the *PurchasePrint* button, the purchase clerk then obtains the *Purchase Data Report* output data, as shown in Figure 7-4.

Purchase Date : 20090230   Purchase No : 001

Supplier : Chao's Corp

ProductNo	Quantity	UnitPrice
A00001	1000	120
A00002	1000	220
A00003	1000	320
A00004	1000	420

Total : 1,080,000

Figure 7-4.   *Purchase Data Report*

Using the structure-behavior coalescence (SBC) approach, we shall go through: a) architecture hierarchy diagram, b) component operation diagram and c) interaction flow diagram, to accomplish the software requirements specification (SRS) 2.0 for the *Purchase System.*

7-1 Architecture Hierarchy Diagram

SRS 2.0 uses an architecture hierarchy diagram (AHD) to specify the multi-level composition and decomposition of the *Purchase System* as shown in Figure 7-5. In the figure, *Purchase_System* is composed of *Presentation_Layer* and *Data_Layer*; *Presentation_Layer* is composed of *PurchaseInput_UI* and *PurchasePrint_UI*; *Data_Layer* is composed of *Purchase_Database.*

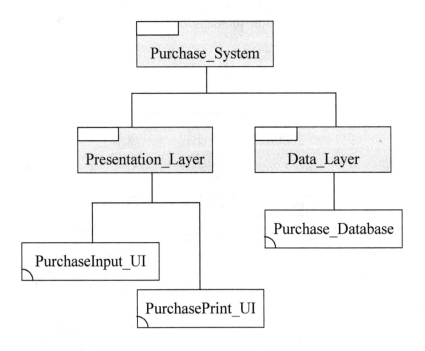

Figure 7-5   AHD of the *Purchase System*

In Figure 7-5, *Purchase_System*, *Presentation_Layer* and *Data_Layer* are aggregated systems while *PurchaseInput_UI*, *PurchasePrint_UI* and *Purchase_Database* are non-aggregated systems.

7-2 Component Operation Diagram

SRS 2.0 uses a component operation diagram (COD) to specify the operations of all components of the *Purchase System* as shown in Figure 7-6. In the figure, component *PurchaseInput_UI* has one operation: *PurchaseDataInput*; component *PurchasePrint_UI* has one operation: *PurchasePrintButtonClick*; component *Purchase_Database* has two operations: *Sql_p_insert* and *Sql_p_select*.

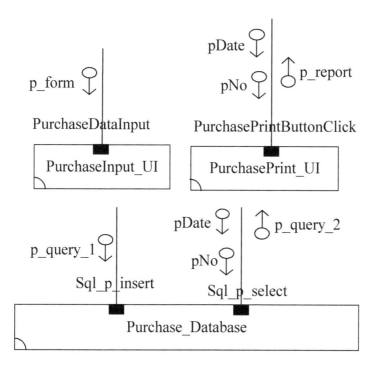

Figure 7-6   COD of the *Purchase System*

The operation formula of *PurchaseDataInput* is *PurchaseDataInput(In p_form)*. The operation formula of *PurchasePrintButtonClick* is *PurchasePrintButtonClick(In pDate, pNo; Out p_report)*. The operation formula of *Sql_p_insert* is *Sql_p_insert(In p_query_1)*. The operation formula of *Sql_p_select* is *Sql_p_select(In pDate, pNo; Out p_query_2)*.

Figure 7-7 shows the composite data type specification of the *p_form* input parameter occurring in the *PurchaseDataInput(In p_form)* operation formula.

Parameter	*p_form*

Data Type	TABLE of
	  Purchase Date : Text
	  Supplier : Text
	  ProductNo : Text
	  Quantity : Integer
	  UnitPrice : Real
	  Total : Real
	End TABLE ;

Instances	**Purchase Input Form**
	
	             Purchase Date:__2010/06/12
	Supplier : _Chao's Corp._
	
	  ProductNo Quantity Unit Price
	  __A00001_____1000_____120.00___
	  __A00002_____2000_____220.00___
	  __A00003_____3000_____320.00___
	  __A00004_____4000_____420.00___
	
	      Merchandise Total : 1,080,000.00

Figure 7-7   Composite Data Type Specification of *p_form*

Figure 7-8 shows the primitive data type specification of the *pDate* and *pNo* input parameters occurring in the *PurchasePrintButtonClick(In pDate, pNo; Out p_report)* and *Sql_p_select(In pDate, pNo; Out p_query_2)* operation formulas.

Parameter	Data Type	Instances
pDate	Text	20110317, 20110412
pNo	Text	003, 004

Figure 7-8   Primitive Data Type Specification

Figure 7-9 shows the composite data type specification of the *p_report* output parameter occurring in the *PurchasePrintButtonClick(In pDate, pNo; Out p_report)* operation formula.

Parameter	*p_report*

Data Type	TABLE of
	   Purchase Date : Text
	   Purchase No : Text
	   Supplier : Text
	   ProductNo : Text
	   Quantity : Integer
	   UnitPrice : Real
	   Total : Real End TABLE ;

Instances	Purchase Date : 20100612 Purchase No : 001 Supplier : Chao's Corp <table><tr><th>ProductNo</th><th>Quantity</th><th>UnitPrice</th></tr><tr><td>A00001</td><td>1000</td><td>120.00</td></tr><tr><td>A00002</td><td>1000</td><td>220.00</td></tr><tr><td>A00003</td><td>1000</td><td>320.00</td></tr><tr><td>A00004</td><td>1000</td><td>420.00</td></tr></table> Total : 1,080,000.00

Figure 7-9   Composite Data Type Specification of *p_report*

Figure 7-10 shows the composite data type specification of the *p_query_1* input parameter occurring in the *Sql_p_insert(In p_query_1)* operation formula.

Parameter	p_query_1

Data Type	TABLE of
	  Purchase Date : Text
	  Purchase No : Text
	  Supplier : Text
	  ProductNo : Text
	  Quantity : Integer
	  UnitPrice : Real
	  Total : Real
	End TABLE ;

Instances

Purchase Date	Purchase No	Supplier	Total
20090230	001	Chao's Corp	1,080,000.00

ProductNo	Quantity	UnitPrice
A00001	1000	120.00
A00002	1000	220.00
A00003	1000	320.00
A00004	1000	420.00

Figure 7-10   Composite Data Type Specification of p_query_1

Figure 7-11 shows the composite data type specification of the p_query_2 output parameter occurring in the Sql_p_select(Out p_query_2) operation formula.

Parameter	*p_query_2*
Data Type	TABLE of 　Purchase Date : Text 　Purchase No : Text 　Supplier :　Text 　ProductNo : Text 　Quantity : Integer 　UnitPrice : Real 　Total : Real End TABLE ;
Instances	

Purchase Date	Purchase No	Supplier	Total
20090230	001	Chao's Corp	1,080,000.00

ProductNo	Quantity	UnitPrice
A00001	1000	120.00
A00002	1000	220.00
A00003	1000	320.00
A00004	1000	420.00

Figure 7-11　　Composite Data Type Specification of *p_query_2*

7-3 Interaction Flow Diagram

The overall behavior of the *Purchase System* includes two individual behaviors: *PurchaseInput*, *PurchasePrint*. Each individual behavior is represented by an execution path. SRS 2.0 uses an IFD to specify each one of these execution paths.

Figure 7-12 shows an IFD of the *PurchaseInput* behavior. First, actor *Purchase Clerk* interacts with the *PurchaseInput_UI* component through the *PurchaseDataInput* operation call interaction, carrying the *p_form* input parameter. Next, component *PurchaseInput_UI* interacts with the *Purchase_Database* component through the *Sql_p_insert* operation call interaction, carrying the *p_query_1* input parameter.

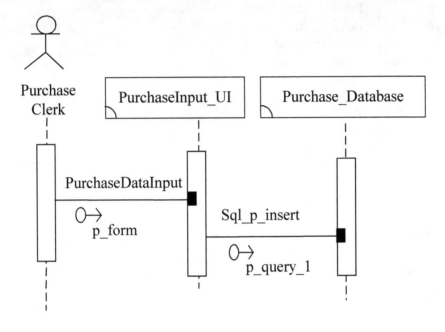

Figure 7-12   IFD of the *PurchaseInput* Behavior

Figure 7-13 shows an IFD of the *PurchasePrint* behavior. First, actor *Purchase Clerk* interacts with the *PurchasePrint_UI* component through the *PurchasePrintButtonClick* operation call interaction, carrying the *pDate* and *pNo* input parameters. Continuingly, component *PurchasePrint_UI* interacts with the *Purchase_Database* component through the *Sql_p_select* operation call interaction, carrying the *pDate* and *pNo* input parameters and the *p_query_2* output parameter. Finally, actor *Purchase Clerk* interacts with the *PurchasePrint_UI* component through the *PurchasePrintButtonClick* operation return interaction, carrying the *p_report* output parameter.

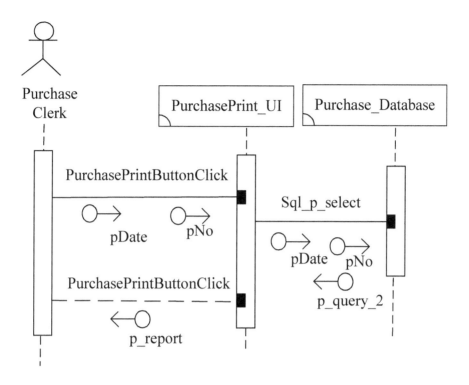

Figure 7-13   IFD of the *PurchasePrint* Behavior

Chapter 8: Software Requirements Specification 2.0 of the Sale System

This chapter examines the *Sale System* which represents a case study of software requirements specification 2.0, using the structure-behavior coalescence approach. After the software development is finished, the overall behavior of the *Sale System* is represented by two behaviors: *SaleInput* and *SalePrint* as shown in Figure 8-1.

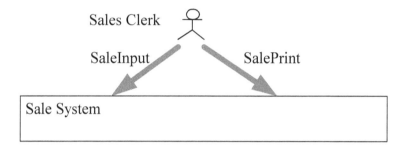

Figure 8-1   Two Behaviors of the *Sale System*

In the *SaleInput* behavior, a sales clerk uses the *SaleInput_GUI* component to input the sale data, as shown in Figure 8-2.

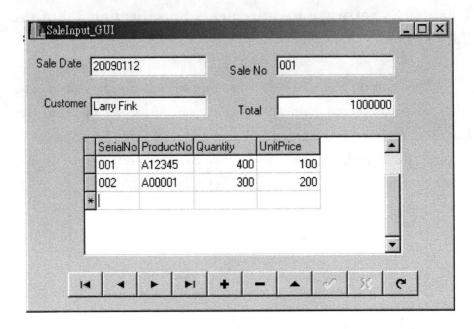

Figure 8-2   Input the Sale Data

In the *SalePrint* behavior, a sales clerk uses the *SalePrint_GUI* component to print out the sale data, as shown in Figure 8-3.

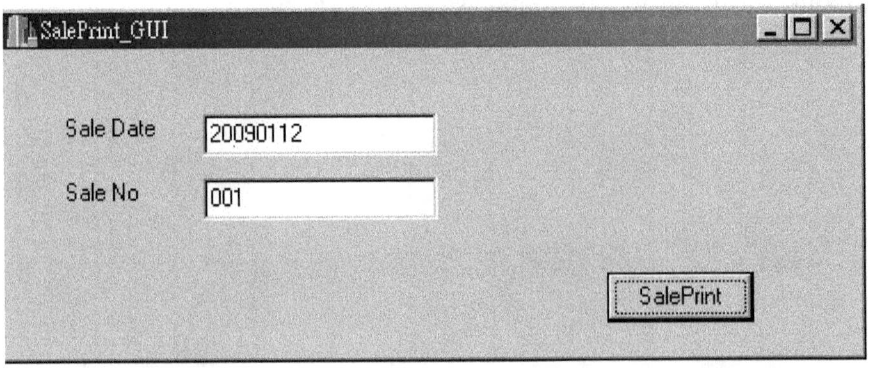

Figure 8-3   Print Out the Sale Data

In Figure 8-3, a sales clerk shall input the *Sale Date* and *Sale No* values first. After pressing down the *SalePrint* button, the sales clerk then obtains the *Sale Data Report* output data as shown in Figure 8-4.

Sale Date : 20090112   Sale No : 001

Customer : Larry Fink

ProductNo	Quantity	UnitPrice
A12345	400	100
A00001	300	200

Total : 100,000

Figure 8-4   *Sale Data Report*

Using the structure-behavior coalescence (SBC) approach, we shall go through: a) architecture hierarchy diagram, b) component operation diagram and c) interaction flow diagram, to accomplish the software requirements specification (SRS) 2.0 for the *Sale System*.

8-1 Architecture Hierarchy Diagram

SRS 2.0 uses an architecture hierarchy diagram (AHD) to specify the multi-level composition and decomposition of the *Sale System* as shown in Figure 8-5. In the figure, *Sale_System* is composed of *Presentation_Layer* and *Data_Layer*; *Presentation_Layer* is composed of *SaleInput_UI* and *SalePrint_UI*; *Data_Layer* is composed of *Sale_Database*.

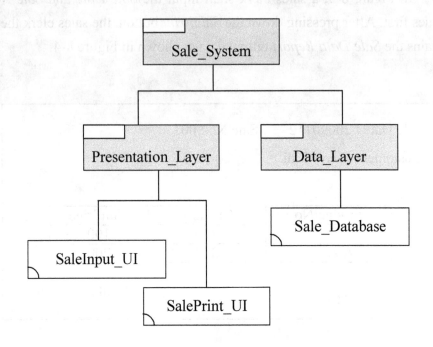

Figure 8-5   AHD of the *Sale System*

In Figure 8-5, *Sale_System*, *Presentation_Layer* and *Data_Layer* are aggregated systems while *SaleInput_UI*, *SalePrint_UI* and *Sale_Database* are non-aggregated systems.

8-2 Component Operation Diagram

SRS 2.0 uses a component operation diagram (COD) to specify the operations of all components of the *Sale System* as shown in Figure 8-6. In the figure, component *SaleInput_UI* has one operation: *SaleDataInput*; component *SalePrint_UI* has one operation: *SalePrintButtonClick*; component *Sale_Database* has two operations: *Sql_s_insert* and *Sql_s_select*.

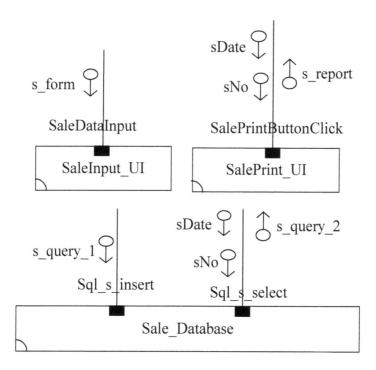

Figure 8-6   COD of the *Sale System*

The operation formula of *SaleDataInput* is *SaleDataInput(In s_form)*. The operation formula of *SalePrintButtonClick* is *SalePrintButtonClick(In sDate, sNo; Out s_report)*. The operation formula of *Sql_s_insert* is *Sql_s_insert(In s_query_1)*. The operation formula of *Sql_s_select* is *Sql_s_select(In sDate, sNo; Out s_query_2)*.

Figure 8-7 shows the composite data type specification of the *s_form* input parameter occurring in the *SaleDataInput(In s_form)* operation formula.

Parameter	*s_form*

Data Type	TABLE of
	   Sale Date : Text
	   Customer : Text
	   ProductNo : Text
	   Quantity : Integer
	   UnitPrice : Real
	   Total : Real
	End TABLE ;

Instances	**Sale Input Form**
	
	                               Sale Date: 2010/05/17
	
	Customer : __Larry Fink__
	
	ProductNo Quantity Unit Price
	
	____A12345_____400_____100.00____
	____A00001_____300_____200.00____
	
	                  Merchandise Total : 100,000.00

Figure 8-7   Composite Data Type Specifications

Figure 8-8 shows the primitive data type specification of the *sDate* and *sNo* input parameters.

Parameter	Data Type	Instances
sDate	Text	20100517, 20100612
sNo	Text	001, 002

Figure 8-8   Primitive Data Type Specification

Figure 8-9 shows the composite data type specification of the *s_report* output parameter occurring in the *SalePrintButtonClick(In sDate, sNo; Out s_report)* operation formula.

Parameter	s_report

Data Type	TABLE of
	   Sale Date : Text
	   Sale No : Text
	   Customer : Text
	   ProductNo : Text
	   Quantity : Integer
	   UnitPrice : Real
	   Total : Real
	End TABLE ;

Instances	Sale Date : 20100517 Sale No : 001 Customer : Larry Fink | ProductNo	Quantity	UnitPrice | |---|---|---| | A12345 | 400 | 100.00 | | A00001 | 300 | 200.00 | Total : 100,000.00

Figure 8-9   Composite Data Type Specifications of *s_report*

Figure 8-10 shows the composite data type specification of the *s_query_1* input parameter occurring in the *Sql_s_insert(In s_query_1)* operation formula.

Parameter	*s_query_1*

Data Type	TABLE of
	   Sale Date : Text
	   Sale No : Text
	   Customer : Text
	   ProductNo : Text
	   Quantity : Integer
	   UnitPrice : Real
	   Total : Real End TABLE ;

Instances	

Sale Date	Sale No	Customer	Total
20090112	001	Larry Fink	100,000.00

ProductNo	Quantity	UnitPrice
A12345	400	100.00
A00001	300	200.00

Figure 8-10   Composite Data Type Specification of *s_query_1*

Figure 8-11 shows the composite data type specification of the *s_query_2* output parameter occurring in the *Sql_s_select(Out s_query_2)* operation formula.

Parameter	*s_query_2*

Data Type	TABLE of
	   Sale Date : Text
	   Sale No : Text
	   Customer : Text
	   ProductNo : Text
	   Quantity : Integer
	   UnitPrice : Real
	   Total : Real
	End TABLE ;

Instances	(see table below)

Sale Date	Sale No	Customer	Total
20090112	001	Larry Fink	100,000.00

ProductNo	Quantity	UnitPrice
A12345	400	100.00
A00001	300	200.00

Figure 8-11   Composite Data Type Specification of *s_query_2*

8-3 Interaction Flow Diagram

The overall behavior of the *Sale System* includes two individual behaviors: *SaleInput*, *SalePrint*. Each individual behavior is represented by an execution path. SRS 2.0 uses an IFD to specify each one of these execution paths.

Figure 8-12 shows an IFD of the *SaleInput* behavior. First, actor *Sales Clerk* interacts with the *SaleInput_UI* component through the

SaleDataInput operation call interaction, carrying the *s_form* input parameter. Next, component *SaleInput_UI* interacts with the *Sale_Database* component through the *Sql_s_insert* operation call interaction, carrying the *s_query_1* input parameter.

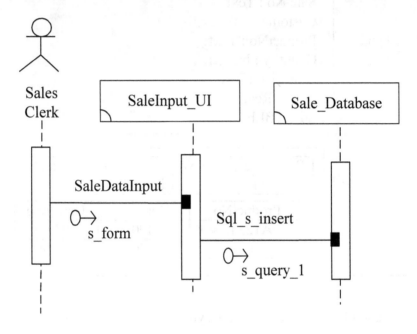

Figure 8-12   IFD of the *SaleInput* Behavior

Figure 8-13 shows an IFD of the *SalePrint* behavior. First, actor *Sale Clerk* interacts with the *SalePrint_UI* component through the *SalePrintButtonClick* operation call interaction, carrying the *pDate* and *pNo* input parameters. Continuingly, component *SalePrint_UI* interacts with the *Sale_Database* component through the *Sql_p_select* operation call interaction, carrying the *pDate* and *pNo* input parameters and the *p_query_2* output parameter. Finally, actor *Sale Clerk* interacts with the *SalePrint_UI* component through the *SalePrintButtonClick* operation return interaction, carrying the *p_report* output parameter.

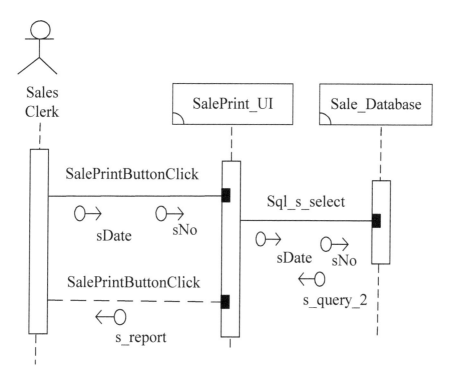

Figure 8-13   IFD of the *SalePrint* Behavior

APPENDIX A: SOFTWARE REQUIREMENTS SPECIFICATION 2.0

(1) Architecture Hierarchy Diagram

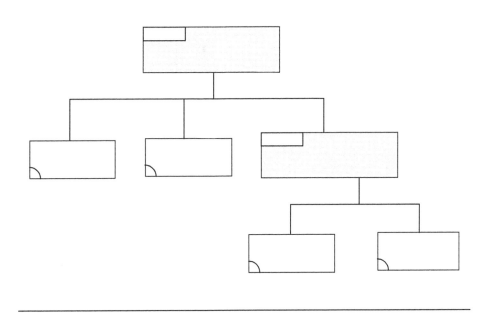

: Aggregated System

: Non-Aggregated System,   Component

(2) Component Operation Diagram

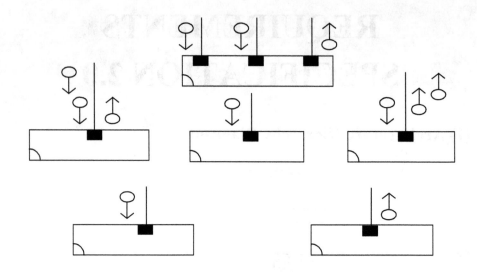

■	: Operation
(input symbol)	: Input Data
(output symbol)	: Output Data
(component box)	: Component

(3) Interaction Flow Diagram

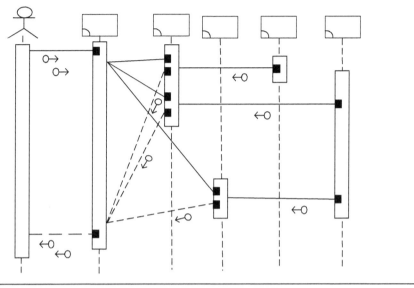

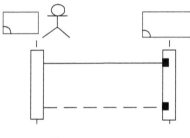

: Operation Call Interaction

: Operation Return Interaction

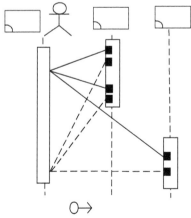

: Conditional
Operation Call Interaction

: Conditional
Operation Return Interaction

: Input Data

: Output Data

APPENDIX B: SBC PROCESS ALGEBRA

(1) Operation-Based Single-Queue SBC Process Algebra

(1) \<System\> ::= **fix(**" \<Process_Variable\> "="\<IFD\> " ● " \<Process_Variable\>
{"+" \<IFD\> " ● " \<Process_Variable\>} ")"

(2) \<IFD\> ::= \<Type_1_Interaction\> {"● " \<Type_1_Or_2_Interaction\>}

(3) \<Type_1_Or_2_Interaction\> ::= \<Type_1_Interaction\>

| \<Type_2_Interaction\>

(2) Operation-Based Multi-Queue SBC Process Algebra

(1) <System> ::= <FixIFD> {"‖ " <FixIFD>}

(2) <FixIFD> ::= **fix**(" <Process_Variable>"="<IFD>
             "●" <Process_Variable> ")"

(3) <IFD> ::= <Type_1_Interaction> {"● " Type_1_Or_2_Interaction>}

(4) <Type_1_Or_2_Interaction> ::= <Type_1_Interaction>

                                      | <Type_2_Interaction>

(3) Operation-Based Infinite-Queue SBC Process Algebra

(1) \<System\>   ::= "! ("\<IFD\> " ● " *STOP* ")" {"|| ! (" \<IFD\> " ● " *STOP* ")"}

(2) \<IFD\> ::= \<Type_1_Interaction\> {"● " \<Type_1_Or_2_Interaction\>}

(3) \<Type_1_Or_2_Interaction\> ::= \<Type_1_Interaction\>

                                | \<Type_2_Interaction\>

BIBLIOGRAPHY

[Ashw90] Ashworth, C., *SSADM : A Practical Approach*, 1st Edition, McGraw-Hill Book Company (UK) Ltd., 1990.

[Bash86] Bashe, C., *IBM's Early Computers*, The MIT Press, 1986.

[Booc07] Booch, G.. et al,. *Object-Oriented Analysis and Design with Applications*, 3rd Edition, Addison-Wesley Professional, 2007.

[Chao14a] Chao, W. S., *Systems Thingking 2.0: Architectural Thinking Using the SBC Architecture Description Language*, CreateSpace Independent Publishing Platform, 2014.

[Chao14b] Chao, W. S., *General Systems Theory 2.0: General Architectural Theory Using the SBC Architecture*, CreateSpace Independent Publishing Platform, 2014.

[Chao14c] Chao, W. S., *Software Modeling and Architecting: Structure-Behavior Coalescence for Software Architecture*, CreateSpace Independent Publishing Platform, 2014.

[Chao15a] Chao, W. S., *Theoretical Foundations of Structure-Behavior Coalescence*, CreateSpace Independent Publishing Platform, 2015.

[Chao15b] Chao, W. S., *Variants of Interaction Flow Diagrams*, CreateSpace Independent Publishing Platform, 2015.

[Chao15c] Chao, W. S., *A Process Algebra For Systems Architecture: The Structure-Behavior Coalescence Approach*, CreateSpace Independent Publishing Platform, 2015.

[Chao15d] Chao, W. S., *An Observation Congruence Model For Systems Architecture: The Structure-Behavior Coalescence Approach*, CreateSpace Independent Publishing Platform, 2015.

[Chao15e] Chao, W. S., *Variants of SBC Process Algebra: The Structure-Behavior Coalescence Approach*, CreateSpace Independent Publishing Platform, 2015.

[Chao17a] Chao, W. S., *Channel-Based Single-Queue SBC Process Algebra For Systems Definition: General Architectural Theory at Work*, CreateSpace Independent Publishing Platform, 2017.

[Chao17b] Chao, W. S., *Channel-Based Multi-Queue SBC Process Algebra For Systems Definition: General Architectural Theory at Work*, CreateSpace Independent Publishing Platform, 2017.

[Chao17c] Chao, W. S., *Channel-Based Infinite-Queue SBC Process Algebra For Systems Definition: General Architectural Theory at Work*, CreateSpace Independent Publishing Platform, 2017.

[Chao17d] Chao, W. S., *Operation-Based Single-Queue SBC Process Algebra For Systems Definition: General Architectural Theory at Work*, CreateSpace Independent Publishing Platform, 2017.

[Chao17e] Chao, W. S., *Operation-Based Multi-Queue SBC Process Algebra For Systems Definition: Unification of Systems Structure and Systems Behavior*, CreateSpace Independent Publishing Platform, 2017.

[Chao17f] Chao, W. S., *Operation-Based Infinite-Queue SBC Process Algebra For Systems Definition: Unification of Systems Structure and Systems Behavior*, CreateSpace Independent Publishing Platform, 2017.

[DeMa79] DeMarco, T., *Structured Analysis and System Specification*, Prentice Hall, 1979.

[Date03] Date, C. J., *An Introduction to Database Systems*, 8th Edition, Addison Wesley, 2003.

[Denn08] Dennis, A. et al., *Systems Analysis and Design*, 4th Edition, Wiley, 2008.

[Dori95] Dori, D., "Object-Process Analysis: Maintaining the Balance between System Structure and Behavior," *Journal of Logic and Computation* 5(2), pp.227-249, 1995.

[Dori02] Dori, D., *Object-Process Methodology: A Holistic Systems Paradigm*, Springer Verlag, New York, 2002.

[Dori16] Dori, D., *Model-Based Systems Engineering with OPM and SysML*, Springer Verlag, New York, 2016.

[Elma10] Elmasri, R., *Fundamentals of Database Systems*, 6th Edition, Addison Wesley, 2010.

[Ghar11] Gharajedaghi, J., *Systems Thinking: Managing Chaos and Complexity: A Platform for Designing Business Architecture*, Morgan Kaufmann, 2011.

[Hoar85] Hoare, C. A. R., *Communicating Sequential Processes*, Prentice-Hall, 1985.

[Hoff10] Hoffer, J. A., et al., *Modern Systems Analysis and Design*, Prentice Hall, 6th Edition, 2010.

[Kend10] Kendall, K. et al., *Systems Analysis and Design*, 8th Edition, Prentice Hall, 2010.

[Lapl13] Laplante, P. A., *Requirements Engineering for Software and Systems*, 2nd Edition, Auerbach Publications, 2013.

[Laue02] Lauesen, S., Software Requirements: Styles & Techniques, Addison-Wesley Professional, 2002.

[Marc88] Marca, D. A. et al., *SADT: Structured Analysis and Design Technique,* McGraw-Hill, 1988.

[Miln89] Milner, R., *Communication and Concurrency*, Prentice-Hall, 1989.

[Miln99] Milner, R., *Communicating and Mobile Systems: the π-Calculus*, 1st Edition, Cambridge University Press, 1999.

[Pele00] Peleg, M. et al., "The Model Multiplicity Problem: Experimenting with Real-Time Specification Methods". *IEEE Tran. on Software Engineering*. 26 (8), pp. 742–759, 2000.

[Prat00] Pratt, T. W. et al., *Programming Languages: Design and Implementation*, 4th Edition, Prentice Hall 2000.

[Pres09] Pressman, R. S., *Software Engineering: A Practitioner's Approach*, 7th Edition, McGraw-Hill, 2009.

[Reis92] Reisig, W., A Primer in Petri Net Design, Springer-Verlag, 1992.

[Rinz09] Rinzler, B., Telling Stories: A Short Path to Writing Better Software Requirements, 1st Edition, Wiley, 2009.

[Seth96] Sethi, R., *Programming Languages: Concepts and Constructs,*

2nd Edition, Addison-Wesley, 1996.

[Shel11] Shelly, G. B., et al., *Systems Analysis and Design*, 9th Edition, Course Technology, 2011.

[Sode03] Soderborg, N.R. et al., "OPM-based Definitions and Operational Templates," *Communications of the ACM* 46(10), pp. 67-72, 2003.

[Somm06] Sommerville, I., *Software Engineering*, 8th Edition, Addison-Wesley, 2006.

[Wieg13] Wiegers, K. et al., *Software Requirements: Developer Best Practices*, 3rd Edition, Microsoft Press, 2013.

[Your99] Yourdon, E., *Death March: The Complete Software Developer's Guide to Surviving Mission Impossible Projects*, Prentice-Hall, 1999.

112

INDEX

A

aggregated system, 53, 54

AHD. *See* architecture hierarchy diagram

architecture hierarchy diagram, 49, 99

B

building block. *See* component

C

COD. *See* component operation diagram

component, 29

component operation diagram, 55, 59, 100

E

entity. *See* component

F

flow chart, 26

function. *See* operation

I

interaction, 21, 22

interaction flow diagram, 61, 101

M

method. *See* operation

model multiplicity, 23

model multiplicity problem, 23

model singularity, 26, 44

multi-level, 51

   composition, 51

   decomposition, 51

multiple models. *See* model multiplicity

   behavior model, 23

   data model, 23

   function model, 23

   structure model, 23

multiple views, 20

   behavior view, 20

   data view, 20

   function view, 20

   structure view, 20

multiple views integrated. *See* software

   requirements specification 2.0

V

V&V. *See* verification and validation

www.ingramcontent.com/pod-product-compliance
Lightning Source LLC
Chambersburg PA
CBHW060158060326
40690CB00018B/4154